Copyright 2022 by Sarah Casey Smith - All right

This document is geared towards providing exact and reliable information in regard to the topic and issue covered. If advice is necessary, legal or professional, a practiced individual in the profession should be ordered. In no way is it legal to reproduce, duplicate, or transmit any part of this document by either electronic means or in printed format. Recording of this publication is strictly prohibited and any storage of this document is not allowed unless with written permission from the publisher. All rights reserved. The information provided herein is stated to be truthful and consistent, in that any liability, in terms of inattention or otherwise, by any usage or abuse of any policies, processes, or instructions contained within is the solitary and utter responsibility of the recipient reader. Under no circumstances will any legal responsibility or blame be held against the publisher for any reparation, damages, or monetary loss due to the information herein, either directly or indirectly. By continuing with this book, readers agree that the author is under no circumstances responsible for any losses, indirect or direct, that are incurred as a result of the information presented in this document, including, but not limited to inaccuracies, omissions and errors. Respective authors own all copyrights not held by the publisher. The information herein is offered for informational purposes solely and is universal as so. The presentation of the information is without contract or any type of guarantee assurance. Readers acknowledge that the author is not engaging in the rendering of legal, financial, medical or professional advice. Please consult a licensed professional before attempting any techniques outlined in this book.

To all, who are in love with food, just like I am.

Table of Content

Table of Content 3
INTRODUCTION 8
   A Short History Guide 9
CUBAN CUISINE 12
   Meat and Seafood 12
   Rice, Beans, and Plantains 13
   Fruits, Vegetables, and other Crops 14
   Bread and Sandwiches 16
   Desserts 17
   Drinks and Beverages 17
   Garnishes and Condiments 19
   Secrets of Cuban Cuisine 19
BREAKFAST 21
      Cuban Croquettes 22
      Cuban Deluxe Sandwich 24
      Cuban French Toast 26
      Cheesy Sandwich Dip 28
      Potato Balls 30
      Guava Pastries 33
      Huevos Habaneros 35
      Delicious Pizza Cubano 37

Plantain Fufu 39

Simple Rice with Egg 41

Boiled Yuca with Garlic Sauce 43

Deviled Crab Croquettes 45

Cuban Tostones 48

MAIN MEALS 50

Ropa Veja (Cuban Shredded Beef) 51

Juicy Cuban Shrimps 54

Chicken Drumsticks with Yellow Rice 56

Pork Roast 58

Egg Stuffed Meatloaf (Pulpeta) 60

Ground Beef Stew with olives (Picadillo) 63

Stuffed Bell Peppers 65

Cuban Polenta 67

Rice with Chicken and Black Beans 69

Vaca Frita 71

Cuban Cube Steak (Bistec Encebollado) 73

Cuban Tamales 75

Breaded Beef Steak 77

Yuca Fries 79

SOUPS AND STEWS 81

Lentil Soup 82

Cuban Mojo Pot Roast 84

    Chicken Soup 86

    Chicken Fricassee 88

    Cuban Ajaico Soup 90

    White Bean Soup 92

    Beef Stew with Potatoes 94

    Noodle Soup with Corn 96

    Black Bean Soup 98

SALADS 100

    Watercress Salad 101

    Typical Cuban Salad 103

    Confetti Salad 105

    Cuban Green Salad 107

    Lettuce and Pineapple Salad 109

DESSERTS 111

    Cuban Pastries (Bunuelos) 112

    Plantain Fries 114

    Guava Shells with Syrup 116

    Sweet Plantain Casserole 118

    Mojito Shortbread Bars 120

    Coconut Balls with Chocolate 122

    Baked Apple Empanadas 124

    Rice Pudding 126

    Pumpkin Flan 128

CUBAN COOKBOOK

INTRODUCTION

Ninety miles off the coast of Florida is the island of Cuba. It was both the first and the last Spanish colony in the region. The food culture has been influenced by Spanish, French, African, Arabic, Chinese, and Portuguese cultures. Characterized primarily by peasant cuisine, Cuban gastronomic culture concerns less with order, timing, and measurements and commonly highlights only a few ingredients and spices, including oregano, garlic, and bay leaf.

The majority of the Cuban dishes are either sautéed or slow-cooked. When it comes to meat, Cubans usually marinate it with citrus juices and roast them over low heat until the perfect tenderness is achieved.

Cuban cuisine is also rich in root vegetables. Yuca and malanga are usually flavored with mojo - a marinade that is made up of olive oil, onions, garlic, lemon juice, water, and cumin.

There are much more secrets of Cuban cuisine that are worth discovering and trying. The next sections will reveal the history of their gastronomy, the flavors of their past, and the taste of their flourishing food culture.

A Short History Guide

The migration of natives from South America marked the birth of authentic Cuban cuisine. These people primarily engage in fishing and hunting to support the growing population. They were later mixed with indigenous farmer tribes, establishing a more refined Cuban food culture. From then on, Cuban cuisine thrived and diversified through the influences brought not only by the Spaniards but also by Africans, Portuguese, British, and Chinese.

During the colonial era, parts of Cuba also emerged as important trading ports. During this time, Havana was considered the most important trading port, through which Spanish invaders passed before moving on to other towns and islands. The Spanish brought cattle and pigs, which they used in their cooking. As a result, Cuban cuisine strengthened its long connections with Spanish cuisine, having its culture, norms, and gastronomy fused with that of Cuba.

With the arrival of African slaves, Cubans were introduced to a variety of new, unique, and interesting foods. Guinea chicken, curries, malanga, and plantains were introduced to the island, eventually leading to the birth of African-Cuban staples like fufu and tostones. Plantains are now served as side dishes on many Cuban tables. Also commonly consumed are fried bananas, cassava, sweet potatoes, beans, lettuce, chicken, pork, beef, and goat.

When Chinese people were brought to Cuba, they continued the work left by the Africans. After several working years, most of them accepted their freedom and returned home, while some decided to stay to settle on the island for good.

They introduced rice to the island, which turned out to be one of the staple foods of Cuba, paired with any dish they served. Pork, rice, and seafood are all staple ingredients from both cultures, resulting in a scrumptious and thrilling culinary fusion experience. These are usually prepared through "La Caja China" (The Chinese Box), which was adapted by Cubans after watching Chinese workers in Havana's Chinatown cook their meals in wooden boxes with the heat on the top, efficiently cooking and softening any meat they wish to serve. This technique remained part of the Cuban food culture and celebrations.

CUBAN CUISINE

As already mentioned, Cuban cuisine has a flavor that you will not encounter in other cuisines. All due to the different impacts from Spanish, French, Portuguese, Chinese and African cuisines, which helped develop and elevate Cuban cuisine to another level. Below are some of the features and essentials of Cuban cuisine and diet that you should learn about.

Meat and Seafood

Cubans are more than just meat consumers; they are actually meat lovers. Their tables never fail to serve a certain type of meat at almost every meal. To be specific, pork is their primary source of protein. Stuffed pork is one of the most common ways to serve and eat meat. It can also be served as lechon asado (roasted pork) or as pan con lechon (pork-stuffed sandwich). These are best paired with a traditional Cuban sauce made out of garlic, paprika, cumin, and oil. Pork is also found in croquets, medianoche, and chorizo. Cubans are deeply in love with pork and would eat it either fried, roasted, in a thick sauce, or on a sandwich.

Beef is another popular type of meat in the Cuban diet. Similarly, it can be served in many different ways. Sirloin can be sliced thinly into palomilla; beef can be shredded and cooked into ropa vieja or fried into frita (burger).

Meanwhile, chicken is best served with rice, pan-fried, or as a soup. Chicken is eaten occasionally because it is not as widely available as pork or seafood. Seafood, on the other hand, is most typically consumed fried or steamed and is added to paella or a seafood stew. Mackerel and canned sardines are also very popular on the island.

Rice, Beans, and Plantains

Black beans and rice are another mainstay of the Cuban diet. They eat rice practically every day for lunch and dinner, usually with some kind of beans, such as mung, black, or red beans. Beans are high in both protein and fiber. It is often served with hefty quantities of black beans and white rice.

In Cuba, plantains, sweet potatoes, yams, and yuccas are also popular. Plantains are all high in fiber, potassium, niacin, and vitamin C and may be found in practically every meal. They can be made by frying them in salt or stewing them in sugar. A favorite appetizer is tostones rellenos or fried plantains loaded with everything from shrimps to meat. Malanga and boniato, both roots identical to that of potato, are also very popular in Cuban cuisine.

Fruits, Vegetables, and other Crops

Cuban population generally consumes just the amount of fruit and vegetables that their bodies require. On the conventional Cuban menu, you will usually find coconut, guava, papaya, bananas, grapefruit, pineapple, and plantains, which are either boiled, consumed plain, or just quickly fried and eaten as a snack.

Aside from these, corn is regarded as another Cuban staple ingredient. Corn is essential in their stews and soups, especially in tamales, which are prepared using corn, chunks of meat, and a variety of Cuban spices, making a thick and creamy paste that is cooked and served wrapped in a corn husk.

Similarly, potatoes are added to soups and stews. If not, Cubans prefer the potatoes prepared as papas fritas, or what is globally known as French fries.

Bread and Sandwiches

To truly appreciate Cuban cuisine, the Cuban mix sandwich is definitely the go-to snack. It is one of the perfect representatives of Cuban classics. This staple food can be perfectly achieved through a perfect blend of roasted pork, ham, Swiss cheese, pickles, mustard, and other spices stuffed into a traditional, crispy, and crusty Cuban bread.

This is comparable to a French baguette, but it is lighter, fluffier, and crispier, which is achieved through the careful and intricate curation of the bread. This is, in fact, a complete meal that Cubans may enjoy any time of the day.

Desserts

A plethora of pastries, cakes, and custards are the faces of Cuban desserts. Typically, these are served at special gatherings and celebrations or simply at meals during the day. These are best paired with coffee.

Drinks and Beverages

Cubans are proud of their strong, sweet, and aromatic coffee, called caffe cubano, which is consumed with fresh milk, as a colada, or as a bucci. If you miss having a sip, you will definitely fail to complete the entire Cuban experience.

Malta is yet another proud representative of Cuban drinks. It is a combination of water, hops, barley, and condensed milk. On the other hand, Cubans also serve plain black coffee with sugar. This is just among the most common beverages on the Cuban table. Other typical beverages include guarapo, café with leche, and several sodas, including Marterva and Pina.

One of the major industries in Cuba is sugarcane plantations. Given this, it is not surprising that Cuba is also a major producer of rum. This century of experience in rum production even led to the birth of the Bacardi distillery on the southern part of the island. Havana was overrun with "rum-tasting" distillery tours during the heyday of the rum craze in the 1950s. In addition to constructing the Havana Bacardi Building, a marvel of Art Deco, in the nation's capital, Bacardi had already created its well-known Hatuey beer brand. Due to the success of the rum industry, other brands have also made a name for themselves, such as Casa Moreno and Havana Club.

Garnishes and Condiments

When it comes to the essential garnishes and condiments, Cuban kitchens require Tabasco sauce, angostura bitters, limes, lemons, black pepper, salt, coarse salt, cocktail olives, pickled onions, oranges, grenadine, horseradish, and maraschino cherries.

Other significant garnishes and condiments are Rose's lime juice, sugar, cranberry juice, pineapple juice, beer, Worcestershire sauce, orange bitters, lemon-lime soda, milk, orange juice, tomato juice, tonic water, ginger ale, etc.

Secrets of Cuban Cuisine

Cuban cuisine does not necessitate any specific cooking skills. Locals employ the very same cooking procedures as the rest of their neighbors. Of course, each meal must be made in a specific method, and yet all of them are traditional.

Cuban food does not have many peculiarities. Thus, most of the dishes may require either boiling, deep frying, braising, stewing, or steaming. A lot of dishes are cooked through for a period of time and seasoned with herbs and spices, making them decent sources of vital nutrients whilst still being low in saturated fat and sugar.

The most crucial tip on how to make a delicious Cuban meal is to prepare and serve each dish with excitement and openness. In fact, every meal must be cooked with the same enthusiasm as before, as feelings and a passion for food can elevate your food to a higher level and provide a unique experience. These will help you learn how to create traditional Cuban food, which will help you feel a connection to Cuba, its history, and its people.

Evidently, Cuban cuisine is one of the best and most distinct cuisines in the world, and it is something that everyone should try at least once in their lives. Instead of simply learning about these wonderful delicacies, you may roll up your sleeves and start preparing them in the comfort of your home!

BREAKFAST

Cuban Croquettes

| Prep time: 10 min | Cook time: 10 min | Servings: 4 |

Croquettes are a staple breakfast for any day of the week. They can be prepared ahead of time and thus perfect for a busy morning.

Ingredients

- *2 tbsp unsalted butter*
- *½ onion, finely chopped*
- *½ cup whole milk*
- *½ cup all-purpose flour - divided*
- *A pinch of nutmeg*
- *Salt and black pepper to taste*
- *1 tsp tbsp dry cooking wine*
- *½ lb. ground ham*
- *2 eggs*

- ½ cup bread crumbs
- Oil for frying

Directions

- Melt the butter in a saucepan over medium-low heat and sauté the onions for 1 minute.
- Stir in the milk, ¼ cup of flour, nutmeg, salt, and pepper to the saucepan.
- Add cooking wine and ham to the sauce and mix well.
- Reduce the heat to low and let the sauce simmer for 5 minutes.
- Let the ham mixture cool to room temperature, then refrigerate overnight.
- Form 3-inch-long logs from the ham mixture and refrigerate for 30 minutes.
- Crack the eggs in a shallow bowl and wish until smooth.
- In a separate bowl, mix the remaining flour and breadcrumbs.
- Dip the croquettes in the egg and then coat them with the bread crumbs mixture.
- Heat the frying oil in a skillet over medium heat.
- Cook the croquettes for about 4 minutes until they are golden brown. Turn in between if necessary.
- Transfer the croquettes to a paper towel-lined platter.
- Serve with your favorite dip and enjoy.

Nutrition-Per Serving: Calories: 374Kcal, Total Fat: 29g, Total Carbs: 14g, Protein: 13g

Cuban Deluxe Sandwich

| Prep time: 45 min | Cook time: 30 min | Servings: 4 |

Nothing is as good as starting your day with a Cuban sandwich. The pork roast layered with ham, cheese, pickles, and mustard gives the sandwich an irresistible taste.

Ingredients

- *1 lb. pork tenderloin*
- *4 sandwich loaves, cut into halves*
- *1 stick of unsalted butter*
- *1 cup yellow mustard*
- *1 lb. honey glazed ham*
- *4 dill pickles, thinly sliced*
- *8 oz Swiss cheese slices*

For the Marinade

- *2 tbsp olive oil*

- 2 tbsp orange juice
- 1 tbsp lime juice
- 1 tbsp light brown sugar
- ½ tbsp salt + ½ tsp black pepper (or to taste)
- ½ tsp of smoked paprika or to taste
- ½ tsp of cumin or to taste
- 2 minced garlic cloves

Directions

- Preheat the oven to 400°F.
- Add all the pork roast ingredients except the tenderloin to a food processor and mix until well combined. Transfer to a bowl.
- Add the pork tenderloin to the marinade and toss to coat. Marinate for 30 minutes. Place the pork tenderloin on a baking sheet and pour over the marinade. Bake for 25 minutes.
- Transfer the pork roast to a cutting board and slice into ¼ -inch thick slices.
- Meanwhile, prepare the sandwiches by rubbing the outer side of each loaf with 1 tbsp of butter. Place them clean side down on a flat surface and spread each piece with 2 tbsp of mustard.
- Layer ¼ of the ham onto each loaf, followed by the pickle slices, pork roast slices, and then cheese.
- Optional: heat the panini maker or a toaster. Press the sandwiches for 5 minutes until golden brown.
- Serve and enjoy!

Nutrition-Per Serving: Calories: 1197Kcal, Total Fat: 54g, Total Carbs: 135g, Protein: 51g

Cuban French Toast

| Prep time: 10 min | Cook time: 20 min | Servings: 4 |

Who said that you have to throw away leftover bread slices? Coat the bread slices with an egg mixture and cook to golden brown perfection. The slices pair well with a cup of hot coffee.

Ingredients

- 1 cup half and half
- 3 eggs
- 2 tbsp honey
- 1 tbsp vanilla extract
- ¼ tbsp cinnamon
- ⅛ tbsp salt
- 4 tbsp butter

- *8 slices of Cuban bread*
- *Maple syrup for serving*

Directions

- In a bowl, add half and half, eggs, honey, vanilla extract, cinnamon, and salt. Mix until well combined with no lumps.
- Melt 1 tablespoon butter in a saucepan over medium heat.
- Dip 2 bread slices in the egg mixture on both sides and place them in the saucepan.
- Cook the slices for about 5 minutes, turning them halfway through cooking, until golden and crunchy.
- Repeat the process for the remaining bread slices.
- Serve the bread sliced with maple syrup or an extra knob of butter over the top.

Nutrition-Per Serving: Calories: 436Kcal, Total Fat: 22g, Total Carbs: 52g, Protein: 8g

Cheesy Sandwich Dip

| Prep time: 10 min | Cook time: 15 min | Servings: 10 |

Who doesn't love a dip? I love it too. This simple Cuban dip tastes awesome and is a good accompaniment to your crusty slices of bread.

Ingredients

- 2 cups gravy mix
- 1 cup of milk
- 1 ½ cup Swiss cheese, shredded
- 5 tbsp dill pickles
- ¼ cup mayonnaise
- 1 tbsp yellow mustard
- 1 cup deli- sliced pork roast, cut into small pieces
- ½ cup ham, cubed

Directions

- Add the gravy and milk to a saucepan and bring the mixture to a boil over medium heat while stirring constantly.
- Reduce the heat to low and let the gravy mixture simmer for 1 minute.
- Stir in cheese, pickles, mayonnaise, and mustard to the gravy and cook for 3-5 minutes.
- Add pork roast and ham to the dip and cook for 1 minute.
- Serve with bread and enjoy.

Nutrition-Per Serving: Calories: 222Kcal, Total Fat: 12g, Total Carbs: 15g, Protein: 14g

Potato Balls

Prep time: 10 min   Cook time: 20 min   Servings: 4

Impress your kids with potato balls at their birthday party. The crispy golden exterior and a toothsome tender inside make each of their bite unforgettable.

Ingredients

- *2 potatoes, peeled and cubed*
- *1 tbsp olive oil*
- *½ lb. ground sirloin*
- *1 onion, finely chopped*
- *1 minced garlic clove*
- *1 green bell pepper, finely chopped*
- *1 red bell pepper, finely chopped*
- *1 tsp Worcestershire sauce (or more to taste)*

- ¼ tbsp sweet paprika
- ¼ tbsp dried oregano
- A pinch of salt and black pepper
- ¼ tbsp cumin
- ½ lime, juiced
- 1 egg
- 1 tbsp water
- 1 tsp warm milk
- ½ cup dry bread crumbs
- ¼ cup all-purpose flour
- Oil for frying

Directions

- Boil the potatoes in a skillet for about 15 minutes until tender.
- Mash the potatoes and set them aside to cool.
- Meanwhile, heat a skillet over medium heat.
- Add 1 tbsp of oil and sirloin to the skillet. Break up the beef using a wooden spoon, and cook for about 5 minutes.
- Stir in the onions, garlic, and bell peppers to the sirloin and cook for 5 more minutes, until the onion is translucent.
- Add Worcestershire sauce, paprika, oregano, salt, pepper, cumin, and lime juice to the sirloin, then cook for 5 minutes.
- Scoop a spoonful of the potato and flatten it using your hand.
- Place a spoonful of the beef mixture at the center of the potato and fold carefully to seal. Repeat the process for all the potato and beef mixture.
- Whisk the egg, milk, and water in a shallow bowl.
- In a separate bowl, mix the flour with bread crumbs.
- Dip the potato ball in the egg mixture, then coat them with the bread crumbs mixture.

- Heat the oil in a skillet over medium heat and deep fry the potato balls for about 5 minutes until golden brown.
- Serve and enjoy.

Nutrition-Per Serving: Calories: 329Kcal, Total Fat: 9g, Total Carbs: 44g, Protein: 19g

Guava Pastries

| Prep time: 30 min | Cook time: 25 min | Servings: 6 |

Guavas are a common fruit in all local markets. Add guava paste to your pastries for a unique and sweeter flavor. Your family will ask you to prepare them more.

Ingredients

- *2 sheets of puff pastry*
- *1 package of guava paste*
- *1 egg*
- *2 tbsp sugar*

Directions

- Preheat the oven to 400°F.
- Unfold the pastry and place it on the cutting board. Cut it into squares. Make about 6 squares out of each, or as you wish.

- Place the guava paste on a cutting board and divide it into as many parts as you have squares, about 12.
- Place one guava part in the middle of each pastry square, then fold it in half so that you have triangles or a rectangle, whatever you prefer. Seal the edges with a fork or with your thumbs.
- Put the pastries on a baking sheet lined with parchment paper or greased with butter.
- In a bowl, whisk the egg and 1 tablespoon of water.
- Brush the puff pastry with the egg wash and sprinkle it with sugar.
- Bake the guava pastry for 20 minutes or until golden on top.
- Let the pastry cool for 10-15 minutes prior to serving it.

Nutrition-Per Serving: Calories: 133Kcal, Total Fat: 8g, Total Carbs: 14g, Protein: 3g

Huevos Habaneros

| Prep time: 20 min | Cook time: 35 min | Servings: 4 |

Impress your family with these huevos habaneros in place of a regular egg breakfast. Baking eggs in tomato sauce give the eggs an incredible flavor that is addictive.

Ingredients

- *2 tbsp olive oil*
- *1 onion, finely diced*
- *1 red pepper, finely diced*
- *3 minced garlic cloves*
- *1 cup tomato sauce*
- *1 cup pimientos: drained*
- *3 tbsp dry white wine*
- *4 eggs*
- *4 tbsp melted butter*

- *Salt and black pepper to taste*
- *1 tbsp chopped parsley*
- *Cherry tomatoes or chili, for serving*

Directions

- Preheat the oven to 350°F.
- Heat the oil in a skillet over medium heat.
- Sauté the onions, pepper, and garlic for 5 minutes.
- Stir in tomato sauce, pimentos, and wine to the onions and cook for 10 more minutes.
- Spoon the sauce into 4 oven-proof bowls.
- Make a well at the center of the sauce and crack an egg on top.
- Drizzle 1 tablespoon of melted butter over each egg and bake for 15 - 20 minutes or until done
- Garnish the eggs with salt, pepper, parsley and chopped chilis or cherry tomatoes and serve.

Nutrition-Per Serving: Calories: 276Kcal, Total Fat: 23g, Total Carbs: 8g, Protein: 8g

Delicious Pizza Cubano

| Prep time: 30 min | Cook time: 20 min | Servings: 4 |

Make this pizza at home and you will never buy it in a store again. It has a sweeter and thicker crust layered with a flavorful topping that you are not likely to find in store-bought ones.

Ingredients

- ½ tbsp active dry yeast
- ½ cup of warm water (or more if needed)
- ¼ tbsp sugar
- 1 ½ cups all-purpose flour
- 1 pinch of salt
- 1 tbsp + ½ tbsp olive oil
- ⅓ cup tomato sauce
- 1 cup Swiss cheese, shredded
- ½ onion, thinly sliced
- ½ cup diced ham

- ½ cup roasted pork, shredded
- ½ cup cucumber pickles
- Dip: mustard

Directions

- Mix yeast, water, and sugar in a small bowl. Let the mixture stand for 10 minutes.
- Add the flour, salt, oil, and yeast mixture to a bowl and mix using an electric mixer.
- Cover the dough and let it rise for 30 minutes.
- Preheat the oven to 450°F.
- Place the dough on a greased baking sheet and flatten it uniformly on the pan.
- Brush the dough with the remaining oil and spread the tomato sauce on top.
- Sprinkle cheese over the dough, then add onions, ham, roasted pork and cheese on top. Put in the oven (bottom shelf).
- Bake the pizza for 15 minutes or until the dough is crispy.
- Serve with mustard on top and enjoy!

Nutrition-Per Serving: Calories: 489Kcal, Total Fat: 15g, Total Carbs: 71g, Protein: 16g

Plantain Fufu

| Prep time: 5 min | Cook time: 20 min | Servings: 2 |

Including plantains in your diet is vital as it is highly loaded with fiber and essential nutrients that the body needs. What is more, mashing the plantains is a unique way of enjoying them. They pair well with any meat you can imagine.

Ingredients

- *4 green plantains*
- *2 cups water*

Directions

- Peel the plantains and cut them into small pieces.
- Add the plantains and water to a blender and process into a smooth puree.

- Pour the plantain puree into a skillet and cook over medium heat for about 10-15 minutes or until a stretchy consistency is achieved. Stir regularly and make sure there are no lumps.
- Let the plantain fufu cool for 5 minutes.
- Serve and enjoy.

Nutrition-Per Serving: Calories: 218Kcal, Total Fat: 0g, Total Carbs: 57g, Protein: 2g

Simple Rice with Egg

| Prep time: 10 min | Cook time: 20 min | Servings: 4 |

Rice with egg is a perfect choice whenever you don't feel like cooking. It requires little effort and time to prepare but still tastes great.

Ingredients

- *2 cups water*
- *1 cup white rice*
- *Salt and black pepper to taste*
- *4 tbsp oil*
- *4 eggs*
- *Garnishes: chili flakes, freshly chopped herbs*

Directions

- Pour water into a saucepan and bring it to a boil.
- Add rice and salt to the boiling water and cook uncovered for about 10 minutes.
- Reduce the heat to low and cook the rice covered for an additional 10 minutes until all water has evaporated.
- Meanwhile, heat 1 tablespoon of oil in a pan over medium heat.
- Crack an egg over the pan and season it with salt and black pepper to taste. Cook the egg for 1 minute.
- Repeat the process for all the eggs.
- Serve the rice with eggs on top, garnished with chili flakes or freshly chopped herbs.

Nutrition-Per Serving: Calories: 267Kcal, Total Fat: 8g, Total Carbs: 37g, Protein: 9g

Boiled Yuca with Garlic Sauce

| Prep time: 10 min | Cook time: 35 min | Servings: 4 |

Boiled yuca is tossed in a garlic citrus sauce to make an appealing and delicious appetizer. The root vegetable can be prepared and refrigerated for later use.

Ingredients

- 1 lb. yuca, peeled and cut into pieces
- 1 tbsp salt
- ½ lb. pork belly, cut into small pieces
- ½ cup olive oil
- 1 onion, sliced
- 8 minced garlic cloves
- ⅓ cup bitter orange juice

Directions

- Add yuca to a skillet and pour enough water to cover them.
- Add ½ tablespoon salt to the yuca and bring it to a boil over medium heat. Let the yuca simmer for 20 minutes or until cooked through.
- Meanwhile, add the pork to a saucepan and fry them until they turn golden brown. Sauté the onion in the same saucepan for 3 minutes.
- Add the oil to the saucepan and bring it to a simmer.
- Stir garlic, orange juice, and remaining salt into the oil and cook for 5 minutes. Once done, puree or mash the sauce into a consistent dish.
- Remove any fibrous cores or pieces from the yuca with a fork.
- Pour the sauce over the yuca and serve.

Nutrition-Per Serving: Calories: 744Kcal, Total Fat: 59g, Total Carbs: 47g, Protein: 7g

Deviled Crab Croquettes

Prep time: 45 min | Cook time: 30 min | Servings: 4

Do you know that you can make croquettes using crab meat? They have a crispy outside and a tender inside that makes you enjoy every bite of it.

Ingredients

- *1 loaf of bread, one day old with crust removed*
- *2 cups water*
- *1 loaf, crushed and sifted*
- *1 tsp sweet paprika*
- *¼ tbsp salt*
- *2 tbsp olive oil*

- *2 finely chopped onions*
- *½ red bell pepper, finely chopped*
- *2 minced garlic cloves*
- *¼ tbsp hot red pepper*
- *2 bay leaves*
- *½ tsp sugar*
- *¼ tbsp salt*
- *½ cup water*
- *3 oz tomato paste*
- *1 lb. crab meat, shredded*
- *1 egg*
- *½ cup milk*
- *Salt to taste*
- *A pinch of black pepper*
- *1 cup seasoned bread crumbs*
- *½ cup all-purpose flour*
- *Oil for frying*

Directions

- Soak 1 loaf of bread in 2 cups of water for 30 minutes in a bowl.
- Squeeze water from the soaked bread and place it in a bowl.
- Add the crushed bread, paprika, and salt to the wet bread and mix until well combined. Refrigerate for 2 hours.
- Prepare the crab meat filling by heating oil in a skillet over low heat. Sauté the onions, bell peppers, garlic, and red pepper for about 5 min. Stir in bay leaves, sugar, salt, water, and tomato paste into the skillet and cook for 20 minutes until most of the water has evaporated. Remove the bay leaves and stir in the crab meat to the filling. Cook for 3 minutes.
- Turn off the heat and let the filling cool for 30 minutes.

- Scoop 3 spoonsful of the bread dough and flatten it using your hands. Add a spoonful of the crab filling to the center of the dough and fold it to seal it. Repeat the process for all the bread dough and filling.
- In a bowl mix the egg, milk, salt, and black pepper. In a separate bowl mix the bread crumbs and flour. Dip the croquettes in the egg mixture, then coat with the bread crumbs mixture.
- Heat the oil in a skillet over medium heat and deep fry the croquettes for 3 minutes on each side. Serve and enjoy.

Nutrition-Per Serving: Calories: 758Kcal, Total Fat: 18g, Total Carbs: 112g, Protein: 40g

Cuban Tostones

| Prep time: 10 min | Cook time: 10 min | Servings: 2 |

Green plantain rounds are fried, flattened then fried again. This makes them sweeter and crispier than bananas - unlike most people think. They are just irresistible.

Ingredients

- *2 cups vegetable oil for frying*
- *2 green plantains, peeled and sliced into 1-inch pieces*
- *Salt to taste*

Directions

- Heat the oil in a skillet over medium heat.
- Deep fry the plantain pieces for about 5 minutes per side until they turn golden brown.

- Transfer the plantain to a plate lined with a paper towel without overlapping.
- Smash each plantain piece using a wooden spoon.
- Deep fry the plantain for an additional minute per side.
- Place the tostones on a paper towel-lined platter and allow them to drain excess oil.
- Sprinkle the tostones with salt and serve with your favorite dip.

Nutrition-Per Serving: Calories: 229Kcal, Total Fat: 18g, Total Carbs: 19g, Protein: 1g

MAIN MEALS

Ropa Veja (Cuban Shredded Beef)

| Prep time: 15 min | Cook time: 4 h 40 min | Servings: 4 |

Do you have a slow cooker in your kitchen? If yes, then you should try this recipe. Though it takes long hours to prepare, the results are worth waiting for.

Ingredients

- *2-3 tbsp olive oil*
- *1 ½ lb. beef chucks*
- *Salt and black pepper to taste*
- *1 yellow onion, thinly sliced*
- *1 bell pepper, thinly sliced*
- *2 minced garlic cloves*

- ½ tbsp dried oregano
- ½ tbsp ground cumin
- ½ tbsp ground paprika
- ½ cup dry white wine
- 1 cup chicken broth
- 8 oz crushed tomatoes
- 2 oz tomato paste
- 2 bay leaves
- 1 carrot, finely diced
- ½ celery stalk, chopped
- ½ cup green olives, rinsed and drained
- ½ cup roasted red pepper, drained
- ¼ cup pimientos, drained
- 2 tsp capers, rinsed and drained
- ⅓ cup chopped parsley (or to taste, for garnish)

Directions

- Dry the beef with a paper towel, then season it with salt and black pepper. Heat the oil in a skillet over medium heat and brown the beef on both sides for about 5 minutes. Transfer the beef to a plate reserving the cooking juices.
- Add the onions and bell peppers to the same skillet and cook for 5 minutes. Stir in garlic and all spices to the bell peppers and cook for 1 minute.
- Add white wine to the skillet and deglaze. Bring the mixture to a boil after adding the broth. Stir in the tomatoes, tomato paste, and bay leaves to the broth and simmer for about 2-3 minutes.
- Add the beef, carrots, and celery to the sauce and let the mixture simmer over low heat for 4 hours.
- Remove the bay leaves from the stew and discard them.

- Transfer the beef to a cutting board and shred it with a fork.
- Stir the beef, olives, roasted peppers, pimientos, and capers back into the pan and cook for another 15 – 20 minutes so that the flavors get together.
- Stir in the parsley to the stew and adjust the seasoning. Add additional salt or black pepper if needed.
- Serve with bread or rice and enjoy.

Nutrition-Per Serving: Calories: 306Kcal, Total Fat: 16g, Total Carbs: 15g, Protein: 25g

Juicy Cuban Shrimps

| Prep time: 10 min | Cook time: 25 min | Servings: 4 |

These juicy shrimps are one of the meals that can be whipped up together easily whenever you feel that you have less energy left. It takes less than 30 minutes to put this meal on the table.

Ingredients

- 2 tbsp olive oil
- ½ onion, finely diced
- ½ green bell pepper, finely diced
- 4 minced garlic cloves
- 8 oz tomato sauce

- ½ cup water
- ½ cup white wine
- ⅓ cup olives
- ⅛ tbsp dried oregano
- Salt and black pepper to taste
- 1 ½ lb. medium-sized shrimps, peeled and deveined

Directions

- Heat the oil in a skillet over medium heat and sauté the onions and peppers for 3 minutes.
- Stir in the garlic and 2 tablespoons of tomato sauce to the onions. Cook for 2 minutes.
- Add the remaining tomato sauce, water, wine, olives, oregano, salt, and pepper to the skillet and cook for 5-10 minutes or until the flavors combine well.
- Add shrimps to the sauce and cook for another 5 minutes, until the shrimps are just done.
- Serve and enjoy.

Nutrition-Per Serving: Calories: 208Kcal, Total Fat: 9g, Total Carbs: 7g, Protein: 25g

Chicken Drumsticks with Yellow Rice

| Prep time: 10 min | Cook time: 35 min | Servings: 4 |

When it comes to a comforting one-pot meal, chicken drumsticks with yellow rice are the right option. Its colorful presentation makes it attractive to everyone.

Ingredients

- *2 tbsp olive oil*
- *4 chicken drumsticks*
- *Salt and black pepper to taste*
- *3 ½ cups chicken broth*
- *1 minced garlic clove*
- *¾ cup of uncooked rice*

- ½ lb. peas cooked
- 2 roasted red peppers, chopped

Directions

- Heat the oil in a skillet over medium-high heat.
- Brown the chicken on both sides for about 5 minutes per side or until the bone is no longer bleeding.
- Transfer the chicken to a plate and season with salt and pepper.
- Pour water into the same skillet and add garlic. Bring the mixture to a boil.
- Add rice to the boiling water and place the chicken on top.
- Cook the rice for about 20 minutes until all the liquid has been absorbed. Stir occasionally.
- Spoon the peas and roasted peppers over the rice and cook covered for 5 minutes.
- Serve and enjoy.

Nutrition-Per Serving: Calories: 354Kcal, Total Fat: 20g, Total Carbs: 8g, Protein: 33g

Pork Roast

| Prep time: 10 min | Cook time: 3 h 5 min | Servings: 6 |

How do you enjoy your Sunday evening? Prepare this delicious pork roast for dinner for your family. It is simple to prepare and an affordable way of giving your family a treat.

Ingredients

- *3 lb. pork shoulder roast, boneless*
- *½ cup orange juice*
- *¼ cup lime juice*
- *¼ cup lemon juice*
- *¾ tbsp dried oregano*
- *¼ tbsp ground cumin*
- *Salt and black pepper to taste*

- *8 minced garlic cloves*
- *½ onion, sliced*

Directions

- Pat dry the pork with a paper towel.
- Add the remaining ingredients to a bowl and mix well.
- Add the pork to the marinade and refrigerate overnight.
- Preheat the oven to 325°F.
- Place the pork on a baking dish with the skin side up.
- Roast the pork for 3 hours, rubbing it with 4 tbsp of the marinade after 1 hour of cooking. Every once in a while, open the oven and pour over the pork the sauces from the bottom of the pan. Once done, put off the oven.
- Add the remaining marinade from the pan to a skillet and simmer for 5 minutes, until a bit thicker.
- Serve the pork roast with the marinade sauce. It pairs well with rice or mashed potatoes.

Nutrition-Per Serving: Calories: 314Kcal, Total Fat: 8g, Total Carbs: 6g, Protein: 52g

Egg Stuffed Meatloaf (Pulpeta)

| Prep time: 15 min | Cook time: 45 min | Servings: 4 |

Many people think that egg-stuffed meatloaf is sophisticated to make. Contrary to that, you only need to split a regular meatloaf and place the eggs at the center, then seal to get this finger-licking dish.

Ingredients

- 2 tbsp olive oil
- 1 minced onion
- 6 minced garlic cloves
- 1 minced red bell pepper
- ½ cup dry white wine
- 1 cup tomato sauce
- 1 cup beef broth (or water)

- *Salt and black pepper to taste*
- *¼ tbsp cumin*
- *2 bay leaves*

For the Meatloaf

- *1 ½ lb. ground beef*
- *1 ½ lb. ground pork*
- *½ lb. ground ham*
- *1 tbsp sweet paprika*
- *Salt and black pepper*
- *¼ tbsp oregano*
- *4 minced garlic cloves*
- *3 eggs*
- *½ cup bread crumbs*
- *3 hard-boiled eggs, peeled*

Directions

- Add all the meatloaf ingredients except the hard-boiled eggs to a bowl and mix well. Shape the meat mixture into a loaf shape.
- Cut the meatloaf and stuff it with the boiled eggs. Cover well with the meat and wrap with foil (or a cloth). Refrigerate for 2 hours.
- Heat the oil in a pan over medium heat. Brown the meatloaf on both sides for about 10 minutes. Transfer to a plate and set it aside.
- In the same skillet, sauté the onions for 5 minutes or until translucent. Stir garlic and red pepper into the onions and sauté for 2 minutes or until fragrant.
- Add wine, tomato sauce, water, salt, black pepper, cumin, and bay leaves to the garlic mixture and bring the mixture to a boil.

- Add the meatloaf to the sauce and simmer for 50 minutes flipping the meatloaf halfway through cooking. Add more broth/tomato sauce if needed to cover the loaf.
- Remove the bay leaves and discard them.
- Slice the meatloaf and serve with the sauce.

Nutrition-Per Serving: Calories: 192Kcal, Total Fat: 14g, Total Carbs: 14g, Protein: 4g

Ground Beef Stew with olives (Picadillo)

| Prep time: 10 min | Cook time: 25 min | Servings: 4 |

This is a simple yet yummy fulfilling dish than can be prepared ahead of time for a busy weeknight dinner. Even better, it pairs well with many different dishes!

Ingredients

- *1 ½ lb. ground beef*
- *Salt and black pepper to taste*
- *½ onion, chopped*
- *2 minced garlic cloves*
- *1 tomato chopped*
- *½ red bell pepper, finely chopped*

- *2 tbsp cilantro*
- *4 oz tomato sauce*
- *¼ tbsp ground cumin*
- *2 bay leaves*
- *¼ cup green olives, chopped*
- *2 cups cooked rice*

Directions

- Add beef, salt, and black pepper to a skillet and cook it over high heat for 5 minutes. Break the meat lump using a wooden spoon.
- Stir in the remaining ingredients to the beef and let it simmer for 20 minutes.
- Serve with rice and enjoy.

Nutrition-Per Serving: Calories: 207Kcal, Total Fat: 9g, Total Carbs: 5g, Protein: 25g

Stuffed Bell Peppers

| Prep time: 10 min | Cook time: 1 h | Servings: 6 |

Do you have picky eaters in your house? Prepare these stuffed peppers for them. The rice, beef, and spice blend pairs well, making a flavorsome meal that they will love.

Ingredients

- *6 large bell peppers, different colors*
- *4 tbsp olive oil*
- *1 lb. ground beef*
- *1 onion, finely chopped*
- *2 minced garlic cloves*
- *2 bay leaves*
- *1 tsp garlic powder*
- *⅛ tbsp onion powder*

- ⅛ tbsp oregano
- Salt and black pepper
- ¼ cup dry white wine
- 1 tbsp tomato paste
- ¾ cup tomato sauce
- ½ cup water
- 3 tbsp olives, chopped
- 3 tbsp raisins
- 1 cup cooked rice

Directions

- Cut off the pepper tops and remove the seeds and membranes. Reserve the tops.
- Heat the oil in a skillet over medium heat and cook the beef for 10 min. Stir in the onions, garlic cloves, bay leaves, garlic powder, onion powder, oregano, salt, and pepper to the beef and cook for 5 more min.
- Stir in the wine, tomato paste, tomato sauce, and water to the beef and cook for 25 minutes.
- Add olives and raisins to the stew and stir. Cook for 5 minutes.
- Turn off the heat and stir in the rice.
- Stuff each bell pepper with the rice mixture and cover with a top.
- Place the stuffed peppers on the baking sheet and bake in the oven for 25 minutes.
- Serve and enjoy.

Nutrition-Per Serving: Calories: 305Kcal, Total Fat: 15g, Total Carbs: 25g, Protein: 15g

Cuban Polenta

| Prep time: 15 min | Cook time: 35 min | Servings: 4 |

Do you have a busy day full of physical activities? Polenta is the breakfast to take. It not only energizes you but also keeps you full till the next meal.

Ingredients

- 2 tbsp + 1 tbsp + 1 tbsp olive oil
- 1 lb. pork meat, boneless, cut into ½-inch cubes
- ½ cup yellow onion, chopped
- ½ cup jalapeno pepper
- 1 garlic clove, chopped
- ½ cup chopped tomatoes

- *Salt and black pepper to taste*
- *4 cups fresh corn kernels*
- *¼ cup chopped parsley*
- *4 lime wedges*

Directions

- Heat 2 tbsp of oil in a skillet over medium heat and brown the pork for 8-10 minutes. Transfer to a plate.
- Using the same skillet, sauté the onions, and jalapeno in 1 tbsp of oil for 5 minutes, until the onion is translucent.
- Add garlic and stir for another minute.
- Stir in the tomatoes and pork to the sauteed onions. Cook for 5 minutes, stirring occasionally until the pork is no longer pink inside.
- Season the pork with salt and pepper and turn off the heat.
- Add the corn kernels to a food processor and process them into a smooth puree.
- Heat the remaining oil in a skillet over medium heat.
- Add the corn puree to the skillet and cook for 15 minutes.
- Stir in the pork mixture to the corn and season to taste with additional salt and black pepper.
- Serve the polenta in bowls, garnished with parsley and lime wedges.

Nutrition-Per Serving: Calories: 272Kcal, Total Fat: 13g, Total Carbs: 27g, Protein: 16g

Rice with Chicken and Black Beans

| Prep time: 20 min | Cook time: 40 min | Servings: 6 |

Black beans are not only rich in protein but also in fiber which is important for a healthy digestive system. Besides, this dish will satiate you on any ravenous day.

Ingredients

- *Cooking spray or oil for greasing*
- *2 ¼ lb. chicken thighs*
- *⅛ tbsp adobo seasoning blend*
- *¼ cup green onion, sliced*
- *2 roasted red pepper, chopped*
- *1 cup white rice, uncooked*
- *8 oz tomato sauce*
- *15 oz canned black beans, drained*

- *1 ½ cup water*
- *1 tbsp chicken bouillon*

Directions

1. Spritz a skillet with cooking spray and heat it over medium-high heat.
2. Season the chicken with the adobo seasoning and cook it for 5 minutes on each side.
3. Remove the chicken from the skillet and set it aside.
4. Add the onions, roasted peppers, and rice to the chicken and cook for 3-4 minutes while stirring constantly.
5. Stir in tomato sauce, beans, water, and bouillon to the rice.
6. Place the chicken over the rice and simmer for 25 minutes until all the liquid is absorbed and the chicken is cooked through.
7. Serve and enjoy.

Nutrition-Per Serving: Calories: 383Kcal, Total Fat: 14g, Total Carbs: 35g, Protein: 25g

Vaca Frita

| Prep time: 10 min | Cook time: 1 h | Servings: 4 |

You don't need to order crispy shredded beef if you can make it at home. This homemade beef is healthier and budget-friendly compared to a store-bought one.

Ingredients

- 1 ½ lb. flank steak
- 2 cups beef broth
- Salt and black pepper to taste
- 1 tsp garlic powder
- 2 tbsp lime juice
- 2 tbsp canola oil

Directions

- Add the steak and beef broth to a skillet and bring the broth to a boil. Cook for 15 minutes.
- Reduce the heat to medium-low and cook for another 30 minutes, turning the steak halfway through cooking.
- Transfer the steak to a cutting board and let it cool slightly.
- Shred the steak so that it resembles thin strings.
- Add the salt, garlic powder, lime juice, and shredded beef to the broth and mix. Cook for a further 5-10 minutes until the liquid somewhat evaporates.
- Brown the shredded beef in the pan for a few more minutes after, until a thick and sticky consistency is achieved.
- Serve with rice, or even better, add to a bun and eat it like a burger!

Nutrition-Per Serving: Calories: 321Kcal, Total Fat: 15g, Total Carbs: 3g, Protein: 38g

Cuban Cube Steak (Bistec Encebollado)

| Prep time: 30 min | Cook time: 15 min | Servings: 4 |

Are you wondering what to prepare for lunch? This recipe is for you. You just need a few pantry ingredients to have this satisfying meal on the table.

Ingredients

- *6 minced garlic cloves*
- *A pinch of oregano*
- *2 tbsp olive oil*
- *¼ cup red wine vinegar*
- *2 lb. cube steak*
- *¼ tbsp adobo seasoning*
- *2 onions, thinly sliced*

Directions

- Add garlic, oregano, oil, and vinegar to a bowl and mix.
- Season the cube steak with adobo seasoning, then place it in the marinade.
- Coat the cube steak with the marinade, then marinate for 2 hours.
- Heat a skillet over medium-high heat.
- Add the steak to the skillet and cook for 3-4 minutes on each side. Add the marinade and cook for a further minute or two.
- In a separate bowl, fry the onions in 1 tbsp of oil for 3-4 min, until translucent and a bit brown.
- Serve the steak, covered with marinade and topped with onions. It pairs well with mashed potatoes or yuca.

Nutrition-Per Serving: Calories: 520Kcal, Total Fat: 32g, Total Carbs: 7g, Protein: 48g

Cuban Tamales

| Prep time: 30 min | Cook time: 1 h | Servings: 6 |

Ground corn, mixed with pork and then cooked in corn husks, is just the finger-licking combination that will come in hand on every picking.

Ingredients

- ¼ cup oil
- ¾ lb. pork, cut into small pieces
- 1 onion, finely chopped
- 3 garlic cloves minced
- 1 red pepper, chopped
- 8 oz tomato sauce
- Salt and black pepper to taste
- 1 ¼ cup chicken broth
- 1 ½ cup ground corn (cooked or canned)

- ¼ *cup butter*
- *1 ¼ cup masa harina*
- *12 corn husks*
- *Water for boiling*

Directions

- Heat the oil in a saucepan over medium heat and fry the pork for 5 min. Add the onions and pork to the mix. Cook for 4 min. Stir in garlic and peppers to the onions and cook for 3 more min.
- Stir in tomato sauce, salt, black pepper, and chicken broth to the pork and simmer for 10 minutes.
- Meanwhile, add the corn, butter, and masa harina to a bowl and mix. Stir in the corn mixture to the pork until well combined. Turn off the heat.
- Divide the corn mixture into 6 parts.
- Place each corn mixture part on 2 corn husks and fold to seal. Secure with a butcher's twine.
- Fill a skillet with halfway water and bring it to a boil.
- Boil the tamales for 30 minutes. Serve and enjoy!

Nutrition-Per Serving: Calories: 528Kcal, Total Fat: 26g, Total Carbs: 49g, Protein: 27g

Breaded Beef Steak

Prep time: 4 h 10 min   Cook time: 10 min   Servings: 4

Beef steaks are soaked in a tangy marinade, then coated with breadcrumbs and fried to crispy perfection. Who would hesitate to enjoy such a delicious meal?

Ingredients

- ¼ cup olive oil
- ¼ cup sour orange juice
- 2 tbsp vinegar
- 1 minced garlic clove
- ¼ tbsp adobo seasoning

- ⅛ tsp dried oregano
- 1 ½ lb. beef steak, cut into strips
- 1 cup all-purpose flour
- 2 egg whites
- 1 cup bread crumbs
- Oil for frying

Directions

- In a bowl, whisk the olive oil, orange juice, vinegar, garlic, adobo seasoning, and oregano.
- Add the steak to the marinade and marinate for 4 hours in the fridge.
- Place the flour, egg white, and bread crumbs in 3 different shallow bowls.
- Coat the steaks in flour, dip them in the egg whites and finally coat them with bread crumbs.
- Heat oil in a frying pan over medium heat.
- Deep fry the steaks for about 4 minutes until golden brown.
- Transfer the fried steaks to a platter lined with a paper towel.
- Serve with ketchup or mayo and enjoy.

Nutrition-Per Serving: Calories: 515Kcal, Total Fat: 24g, Total Carbs: 31g, Protein: 42g

Yuca Fries

| Prep time: 10 min | Cook time: 45 min | Servings: 6 |

Boiling the yuca is the common way of cooking the starchy tuber. However, frying it makes it crispy and much tastier!

Ingredients

- 1 ½ lb. fresh yuca, peeled and cut into ½-inch sticks
- ½ tbsp salt
- 2 cups water
- Cooking spray
- 3 tbsp olive oil
- 2 tbsp finely chopped onion
- ¼ tbsp ground cumin

- 6 minced garlic cloves
- 2 tbsp low-sodium chicken broth
- 3 tbsp lime juice
- ¼ tbsp orange juice
- A pinch of black pepper (or to taste)
- 2 tbsp chopped parsley (or to taste)
- Lime wedges (for garnishing)

Directions

- Place the yuca and half of the salt in a skillet, cover with water and cook over medium heat for about 10 minutes. Do not cook it through completely.
- Drain, pat dry with a paper towel and lay on a baking sheet.
- Preheat the oven to 450°F.
- Spritz the yuca with cooking spray, put in the oven and bake for about 20-30 min, tossing or turning the pieces halfway through, until they are golden brown.
- Meanwhile, heat the olive oil in a saucepan over medium heat.
- Sauté onion, cumin, and garlic for 2 minutes.
- Add the chicken broth and juices to the onions and cook for 2 minutes. Turn off the heat and stir in the remaining salt and pepper. Taste and adjust the seasoning.
- Serve the yuca fries with the sauce, garnish with freshly chopped parsley and lime wedges and enjoy.

Nutrition-Per Serving: Calories: 262Kcal, Total Fat: 9g, Total Carbs: 44g, Protein: 2g

SOUPS AND STEWS

Lentil Soup

| Prep time: 10 min | Cook time: 40 min | Servings: 6 |

Did you know that you should never lack lentils in your pantry? They make a hearty soup that not only fulfills you but also improves your digestive system.

Ingredients

- ¼ cup extra-virgin olive oil
- 1 yellow onion, chopped
- 1 green pepper, deseeded and chopped
- 1 carrot, peeled and chopped
- 4 minced garlic cloves
- ¼ tbsp dried oregano
- ⅛ tbsp cumin

- *1 bay leaf*
- *Salt and black pepper to taste*
- *8 cups vegetable broth*
- *3 tbsp tomato paste*
- *1 lb. ham hock (or sausages for cooking)*
- *14 oz brown lentils, rinsed*
- *1 potato, peeled and cubed*
- *1 sweet potato, peeled and cubed*
- *Garnishes: freshly chopped herbs (basil, parsley, thyme)*

Directions

- Heat the oil in a skillet over medium heat.
- Sauté the onion, green pepper, and carrots for 4 minutes. Add garlic to the onion and cook for another minute.
- Stir in oregano, cumin, bay leaf, salt, and pepper to the onions and cook for 3 minutes.
- Add the broth, tomato paste, ham hock, and lentils to the skillet and bring the mixture to a boil. Simmer for 10 minutes.
- Add the potatoes to the soup and cook for 20 minutes.
- Remove the bay leaves and discard them.
- Serve the soup immediately, garnished with freshly chopped herbs if desired.

Nutrition-Per Serving: Calories: 302Kcal, Total Fat: 9g, Total Carbs: 40g, Protein: 21g

Cuban Mojo Pot Roast

| Prep time: 10 min | Cook time: 3 h 10 | Servings: 6 |

You don't have to go to a restaurant to enjoy a savory meal. The citrus and garlic marinade makes the beef tender while at the same time making the meal yummy.

Ingredients

- 2 tbsp orange juice
- 2 tbsp lime juice
- ½ tbsp cumin
- ½ tbsp dried oregano
- ⅛ tsp red pepper flakes
- 4 minced garlic cloves
- 2 lb. beef chuck roast
- Salt and black pepper to taste

- 2 tbsp canola oil
- 2 bay leaves
- ½ lb. carrots, peeled and chopped
- 2 lb. potatoes, peeled and chopped
- 3 cups beef broth
- Chopped parsley for garnishing

Directions

1. Preheat the oven to 325°F.
2. Whisk orange juice, lime juice, cumin, oregano, red pepper flakes, and garlic in a bowl.
3. Season the beef with salt and pepper.
4. Heat the oil in a skillet over medium heat and brown the beef for 5 minutes on each side.
5. Stir in the carrots, potatoes, juice mixture, bay leaves, and broth to the beef.
6. Cook the beef roast over low heat for about 3 hours. Add more broth if it evaporated too soon.
7. Garnish the beef stew with parsley and serve with bread or rice if desired.

Nutrition-Per Serving: Calories: 371Kcal, Total Fat: 19g, Total Carbs: 22g, Protein: 29g

Chicken Soup

| Prep time: 15 min | Cook time: 30 min | Servings: 6 |

Chicken soup is the most appetizing soup that you can ever come across. Besides, it is loaded with many nutrients that will nourish you.

Ingredients

- *1 lb. chicken breast*
- *2 tbsp olive oil*
- *1 yellow onion, chopped*
- *1 ½ cups chopped carrots*
- *4 minced garlic cloves*
- *2 cups potatoes, cubed*
- *6 cups chicken stock*

- 1 tbsp tomato paste
- ¼ tbsp dried oregano
- 1 bay leaf
- 1-2 tsp of each salt and freshly ground black pepper
- 6 oz dried thin spaghetti noodles
- 1 lemon, juiced
- Garnishes: freshly chopped green onions

Directions

- Add the chicken to an instant pot and sauté for about 3 minutes on each side. Transfer to a plate and set it aside.
- Add the oil and onions to the pot and sauté for 4 minutes.
- Add the carrots and potatoes and cook for 3 minutes.
- Stir in garlic to the carrots and cook for 30 seconds.
- Stir in the chicken stock, tomato paste, oregano, bay leaf, chicken, salt, and pepper to the pot and close the lid. Cook for 8 minutes.
- Remove the bay leaf and chicken from the soup. Discard.
- Shred the chicken using a fork and add it back to the pot.
- Add the noodles and lemon juice to the soup and cook for 7 more minutes. Taste and adjust the seasoning if necessary.
- Serve, garnish with freshly chopped green onions and enjoy.

Nutrition-Per Serving: Calories: 317Kcal, Total Fat: 11g, Total Carbs: 36g, Protein: 19g

Chicken Fricassee

| Prep time: 20 min | Cook time: 1 h | Servings: 6 |

Incorporating olives into this stew adds a unique flavor that will make this dish your favorite. The meal is fulfilling on its own but can also be served with mashed potatoes or bread.

Ingredients

- 8 chicken thighs, boneless, cut into small pieces
- 2 cups mojo marinade
- Salt to taste
- ¼ cup olive oil
- 1 yellow onion, diced
- 1 green pepper, diced
- 4 minced garlic cloves

- ¾ cup dry white cooking wine
- 4 cups tomato sauce
- ¼ tbsp oregano
- ¼ cup olives, chopped
- ⅛ tbsp ground cumin
- 2 ½ cups chicken broth
- ¼ cup water
- 2 potatoes, peeled and diced
- ½ cup chopped green onions

Directions

- Add the chicken and mojo marinade to a bowl. Marinate for at least 4 hours. Remove the chicken from the marinade and pat dry it with a paper towel. Season the season with salt.
- Heat the oil in a skillet over high heat and brown the chicken for about 2 min on each side.
- Transfer the chicken to a plate and set it aside.
- Sauté the onions and green peppers in the same skillet for 3 min. Stir in garlic to the onions and cook for another min.
- Add wine to the onion mixture and deglaze for a minute, then add the remaining ingredients except for green onions.
- Simmer for 30 minutes until all the vegetable is cooked through. Garnish the chicken stew with onions and serve.

Nutrition-Per Serving: Calories: 911Kcal, Total Fat: 67g, Total Carbs: 39g, Protein: 38g

Cuban Ajaico Soup

Prep time: 10 min | Cook time: 1 h | Servings: 6

Warm up with this delicious and healthy soup. It is perfect for a light lunch and will help you utilize leftover foods in your house.

Ingredients

- 2 tbsp canola oil
- 1 lb. chicken breast, boneless, skinless
- 4 cups chicken stock
- 2 white onions, peeled and quartered
- 2 minced garlic cloves
- 1 cup potatoes, peeled and cubed
- 1 cup sweet potatoes, peeled and cubed
- 1 cup pumpkin, peeled and cubed

- *2 corn ears, cut into 3 pieces each*
- *1 yellow bell pepper, sliced*
- *1 ripe plantain, peeled and sliced*
- *1 celery rib, chopped*
- *1 carrot, chopped*
- *2 cups water*
- *Salt and black pepper to taste*

Directions

- Heat the oil in a skillet over medium heat and brown the chicken for 6 minutes.
- Add chicken stock, onion, garlic, potatoes, sweet potatoes, pumpkin, corn and bell pepper to the chicken and cook for 30 minutes.
- Remove the chicken from the skillet and let it cool for 10 minutes. Shred it using a fork, then set it aside.
- Stir in the remaining ingredients to the soup. Cook for another 10 minutes.
- Reintroduce the chicken back to the soup and add water. Simmer for another 5-10 min or until all the ingredients are well cooked.
- Adjust the seasoning, divide between the bowls and serve.

Nutrition-Per Serving: Calories: 253Kcal, Total Fat: 4g, Total Carbs: 37g, Protein: 20g

White Bean Soup

| Prep time: 15 min | Cook time: 2 h | Servings: 4 |

Many people think of bean soup as boring soup. Contrary to this, white bean soup taste and smells amazing. It is budget-friendly and requires little energy to prepare.

Ingredients

- *1 lb. white beans, soaked overnight*
- *10 cups of water*
- *2 bay leaves*
- *6 oz salt pork*
- *2 ham hocks*
- *¼ cup olive oil*
- *1 onion, minced*

- *4 minced garlic cloves*
- *¼ tbsp ground cumin*
- *½ tbsp dried oregano*
- *Salt and black pepper to taste*
- *Fresh parsley or cilantro, for garnish*

Directions

- Rinse and drain the beans that have soaked overnight.
- Add the beans, water, bay leaves, salt pork, and ham hocks to a skillet, then bring the mixture to a boil over medium heat.
- Reduce the heat to low and let the soup simmer for 1 ½ hour.
- Remove the salt pork and bay leaves. Discard them.
- Remove the ham hocks from the soup and separate the meat from the bones. Add the meat back to the soup.
- Heat the oil in a skillet over medium heat, then sauté the onions and garlic for 3 minutes.
- Stir in the onions, cumin, oregano, salt, and pepper to the soup and simmer for a further 15 minutes.
- Divide between the bowls, garnish with parsley and serve.

Nutrition-Per Serving: Calories: 449Kcal, Total Fat: 35g, Total Carbs: 22g, Protein: 14g

Beef Stew with Potatoes

| Prep time: 15 min | Cook time: 30 min | Servings: 4 |

This is the ultimate comforting food for a cold day. The beef chunks and potatoes are cooked till tender in a thick creamy sauce resulting in a flavorful stew. Serve the beef stew with pasta or rice.

Ingredients

- *1 ½ lb. beef chuck roast, cut into 1-inch pieces*
- *Salt and black pepper to taste*
- *2 tbsp oil*
- *4 tomatoes, chopped*
- *1 tsp tomato paste*
- *1 cup tomato sauce*
- *1 large white onion, chopped*
- *2 garlic cloves, chopped*

- *3 cups chicken broth*
- *4 potatoes, peeled and cut into pieces*
- *½ cup chopped cilantro (for garnishing)*

Directions

- Season the beef with salt and pepper.
- Heat the oil in a skillet over medium-high heat and cook the beef for 10 minutes, stirring constantly to brown the pieces evenly.
- Meanwhile, add the tomatoes, onion, garlic, tomato paste, tomato sauce and chicken broth to a blender and process into a smooth puree.
- Stir the tomato puree and potatoes into the beef and simmer for 15-20 minutes, until the potatoes are cooked through.
- Stir in cilantro to the beef stew and serve.

Nutrition-Per Serving: Calories: 465Kcal, Total Fat: 27g, Total Carbs: 20g, Protein: 37g

Noodle Soup with Corn

| Prep time: 15 min | Cook time: 1 h 30 | Servings: 4 |

I love preparing healthy and hearty soups for my family. This noodle soup has all the healthy ingredients that my kids love. They never get enough of it.

Ingredients

- 12 cups water
- 2 lb. chicken, bone-in
- 2 cups corn, uncooked
- 2 minced garlic cloves
- 4 cups chicken bouillon
- 2 tbsp sofrito
- Salt and pepper to taste

- ½ lb. angel hair pasta

Directions

- Add water and chicken to a skillet and bring the mixture to a boil over medium heat. Cook for 45 minutes or until the chicken is thoroughly cooked.
- Remove the chicken from the soup and let it cool for 10 minutes.
- Chop the chicken into small pieces, remove the skin and bones.
- Stir in the chicken, corn, garlic, bouillon, sofrito, salt, and pepper to the soup. Cook for 30 minutes.
- Add the pasta to the soup and cook for 5 minutes or until the pasta is done.
- Serve and enjoy.

Nutrition-Per Serving: Calories: 318Kcal, Total Fat: 1g, Total Carbs: 65g, Protein: 11g

Black Bean Soup

| Prep time: 15 min | Cook time: 2 h 5 min | Servings: 6 |

This is a frugal way of feeding a hungry crowd. The soup is quite flavorsome and comforting enough for lunch. You only need a few basic pantry staples to have the soup on the table.

Ingredients

- 2 ½ cups black beans, soaked overnight
- 2 tbsp olive oil
- 1 onion, finely chopped
- 1 red pepper, chopped
- 2 finely chopped garlic cloves
- 1 tbsp dried oregano
- 1 tbsp ground cumin

- *4 bay leaves*
- *1 cup white wine*
- *3 cups chicken broth*
- *2 cups tomato puree*
- *2 tbsp soy sauce*
- *1 tbsp sugar*
- *1 chorizo sausage, sliced*
- *Salt and black pepper to taste*
- *Fresh parsley sprigs for garnishing*

Directions

- Rinse and dry the black beans.
- Heat the oil in a skillet over medium heat.
- Sauté the onion and red pepper for 4 minutes.
- Stir in the garlic, oregano, cumin, and bay leaves to the onions and sauté them for 1 minute.
- Stir in the black beans and wine to the onion mixture and cook for 2 minutes.
- Add the broth, tomato puree, soy sauce, sugar, sausage, salt, and black pepper to the black beans and bring the mixture to a boil.
- Reduce the heat to low and simmer for 2 hours.
- Adjust the seasoning, then serve, garnished with parsley and enjoy.

Nutrition-Per Serving: Calories: 390Kcal, Total Fat: 9g, Total Carbs: 48g, Protein: 19g

SALADS

Watercress Salad

| Prep time: 15 min | Cook time: 20 min | Servings: 4 |

Impress your guests with this light and refreshing salad at your birthday party. The avocado adds a creamy texture, while the watercress adds crunch to the salad.

Ingredients

- 1 ½ lb. pineapple, peeled and cut into small slices
- ½ tbsp sugar
- 2 finely chopped garlic cloves
- 2 tbsp extra virgin olive oil
- 1 tbsp fresh lime juice
- A pinch of ground cumin
- ¼ tbsp salt and black pepper (or to taste)

- *2 bunches of watercress, cleaned (or arugula)*
- *1 avocado, cut into slices*
- *1 red onion, thinly sliced*

Directions

- Place the pineapple on a baking sheet and sprinkle with sugar.
- Broil the pineapple 4 inches from the heat source for 20 minutes turning it halfway through cooking.
- In a bowl whisk the garlic, olive oil, lime juice, cumin, salt, and pepper.
- Add the watercress and ½ of the dressing to a bowl and toss to mix.
- Add the avocado, pineapple, and remaining dressing to the watercress and toss to mix.
- Garnish the salad with onions and serve.

Nutrition-Per Serving: Calories: 159Kcal, Total Fat: 7g, Total Carbs: 26g, Protein: 1g

Typical Cuban Salad

| Prep time: 20 min | Cook time: 0 min | Servings: 4 |

Salads are a great addition to any main meal. However, this Cuban salad is fulfilling enough to be taken as a meal on its own. Even better, no cooking is required.

Ingredients

- 2 heads of romaine lettuce, chopped
- 4 tomatoes, cut into wedges
- 2 avocados, peeled, pitted, and cubed
- 1 red onion, thinly sliced
- 15 ½ oz canned black beans, rinsed and drained

For the Dressing

- ¼ cup lime juice

- ¼ tbsp honey
- 1 minced garlic clove
- A pinch of ground cumin
- Salt and black pepper to taste
- ½ cup extra-virgin olive oil

Directions

- Add the lettuce, tomatoes, avocado, onion, and black beans to a bowl and toss to mix.
- In a separate bowl, whisk all the dressing ingredients until well combined.
- Pour the dressing over the salad and toss to mix.
- Serve and enjoy.

Nutrition-Per Serving: Calories: 536Kcal, Total Fat: 44g, Total Carbs: 34g, Protein: 9g

Confetti Salad

| Prep time: 10 min | Cook time: 40 min | Servings: 4 |

Anything that includes sweet potatoes is delicious. This confetti salad is not an exception. Roasting the vegetable adds more natural sweetness to the salad.

Ingredients

- *14 oz sweet potatoes, peeled and cut into cubes*
- *½ tbsp Cajun seasoning*
- *Salt and black pepper to taste*
- *2 tbsp extra virgin olive oil (divided)*
- *½ cup corn*
- *½ red onion, chopped*
- *10 oz canned red kidney beans, rinsed and drained*
- *1 lime, grated and juice reserved*
- *½ tomato, chopped*
- *5 oz feta cheese, cubed*

- *½ bunch parsley*

Directions

- Preheat the oven to 390°F.
- Add the sweet potatoes to an oven dish and season them with Cajun spice, salt, and pepper.
- Pour 1 tbsp of oil over the sweet potatoes and toss to coat.
- Put in the oven and bake the sweet potatoes for about 30 minutes or until they are tender.
- Heat the remaining oil in a skillet over medium heat.
- Add the corn and onions to the skillet and cook for 5 minutes.
- Stir kidney beans, lime zest, lime juice, and tomatoes into the corn and cook for 1 minute while tossing regularly.
- Add the sweet potato, cheese, and parsley to the corn mixture and stir.
- Serve and enjoy.

Nutrition-Per Serving: Calories: 306Kcal, Total Fat: 12g, Total Carbs: 39g, Protein: 11g

Cuban Green Salad

| Prep time: 10 min | Cook time: 10 min | Servings: 4 |

This green salad is a perfect side that pairs well with almost every meal. Even more, it's healthy and nutritious.

Ingredients

- ½ cup canola oil
- 2 red onions, thinly sliced
- ⅔ cup sherry vinegar
- 3 tbsp fresh lime juice
- Salt and black pepper to taste
- ½ cup extra-virgin olive oil
- 4 tomatoes, chopped
- 4 avocados, cut into cubes
- 3 head romaine lettuce, chopped

Directions

- Heat ¼ cup of canola oil in a skillet over medium heat and sauté the onions for 5 minutes.
- Add ½ of the vinegar to the onions, toss to coat and remove from the heat to cool.
- In a bowl whisk the remaining vinegar, lime juice, salt, black pepper, remaining canola oil, and olive oil until they are well combined.
- Add the onions, tomatoes, avocado, lettuce, black beans, and the dressing to a salad bowl and toss to mix.
- Serve with toasted bread and enjoy.

Nutrition-Per Serving: Calories: 476Kcal, Total Fat: 35g, Total Carbs: 35g, Protein: 11g

Lettuce and Pineapple Salad

| Prep time: 15 min | Cook time: 0 min | Servings: 6 |

Pineapples are the most refreshing fruit in a salad. In addition, they add a sweet taste to this crowd-pleasing salad.

Ingredients

- *2 avocados, peeled and chopped*
- *1 head romaine lettuce, chopped*
- *1 red onion, sliced*
- *1 pineapple, peeled and chopped*

For the Dressing

- *½ cup olive oil*

- *¼ cup lemon juice*
- *2 tbsp honey*
- *½ tsp cumin*
- *Salt to taste*

Directions

- Add the avocado, lettuce, onion, jalapeno, and pineapple to a salad bowl.
- Whisk all the dressing ingredients in a separate bowl until well combined.
- Add the dressing to the salad and toss to mix.
- Serve and enjoy.

Nutrition-Per Serving: Calories: 385Kcal, Total Fat: 28g, Total Carbs: 36g, Protein: 4g

DESSERTS

Cuban Pastries (Bunuelos)

| Prep time: 30 min | Cook time: 20 min | Servings: 8 |

There is no better way of creating an amusement park at your home than by preparing these Cuban pastries. They are quick and easy to prepare.

Ingredients

- *1 cup flour*
- *¼ tbsp salt*
- *⅛ tbsp baking soda*
- *2 egg yolk*
- *2 cups yuca, cooked and ground*

- 2 cups malanga, cooked and ground
- ½ tbsp anise flavoring
- 2 tbsp lemon juice
- Oil for frying

Directions

- Add the flour, salt, and baking soda to a bowl and mix.
- Add the egg yolks, yuca, malanga, and anise flavor to the flour mixture and mix.
- Divide the dough into 8 parts.
- Roll out the dough parts into long strands, then fold them to the desired shapes.
- Heat the oil in a skillet over medium heat.
- Deep fry the pastry for about 4 minutes until golden brown – turn in between.
- Transfer the bunuelos to a paper towel-lined platter.
- Drizzle the bunuelos with maple syrup or cover with sugar and serve.

Nutrition-Per Serving: Calories: 329Kcal, Total Fat: 3g, Total Carbs: 69g, Protein: 7 g

Plantain Fries

| Prep time: 10 min | Cook time: 10 min | Servings: 2 |

There are different ways of preparing plantains. However, frying plantains creates sweet chips that are crispy on the outside and soft on the inside. Try these fried plantains and this will become your favorite way of enjoying them.

Ingredients

- *2 ripe plantains*
- *Oil for frying*

Directions

- Peel the plantains and slice them into small pieces.
- Heat the oil in a skillet over medium heat. Once extremely hot, lay the plantain pieces in the skillet.

- Cook the plantains for about 4 minutes until golden brown.
- Transfer the plantains to a platter lined with a paper towel.
- Serve and enjoy.

Nutrition-Per Serving: Calories: 145Kcal, Total Fat: 1g, Total Carbs: 38g, Protein: 1g

Guava Shells with Syrup

| Prep time: 20 min | Cook time: 20 min | Servings: 4 |

Guavas is one of the nutrients dense fruits that everyone should try. Each bite of these guava shells is yummy and unforgettable. Try them and thank me later.

Ingredients

- 4 ripe guavas, peeled and halved
- 2 cinnamon sticks
- 4 cloves
- 2 Star anise
- 4 cups of water
- 2 tbsp white sugar
- 4 prunes
- ¼ tbsp vanilla extract

Directions

- Remove the guava seed using a tablespoon. Preserve the guava shells.
- Add the guava seeds, cinnamon, cloves, star anise, and water. Boil for 10 minutes. Strain the liquid and discard the solids.
- Add the peeled guava shells, sugar, prunes, and vanilla to the strained liquid and cook them for 10 minutes.
- Let the guava shell cool completely, then serve.

Nutrition-Per Serving: Calories: 160Kcal, Total Fat: 1g, Total Carbs: 37g, Protein: 4g

Sweet Plantain Casserole

| Prep time: 10 min | Cook time: 1 h | Servings: 6 |

Did you find plantain in your local store? Make this a hearty dessert for your kids. They will come back to you for more.

Ingredients

- *6 tbsp unsalted butter*
- *½ cup raisins*
- *1 tbsp brandy*
- *8 ripe plantains, peeled*
- *½ cup brown sugar*
- *½ cup pecans*
- *Garnish: powdered sugar or sugar*

Directions

- Preheat the oven to 350°F.
- Add 4 tablespoons of butter, raisins, and brandy to a bowl and let the raisins increase in size.
- Add 2 tablespoons of butter to a casserole dish and arrange the bananas on top. Sprinkle with sugar and pour the raisin mixture.
- Spread all the pecans all over the dish.
- Bake the bananas for 20-30 minutes, until soft and juicy.
- Serve, sprinkled with extra sugar or powdered sugar and enjoy.

Nutrition-Per Serving: Calories: 416Kcal, Total Fat: 22g, Total Carbs: 56g, Protein: 3g

Mojito Shortbread Bars

| Prep time: 10 min | Cook time: 40 min | Servings: 8 |

A delicious layer of shortbread is covered with a yummy creamy layer that melts in your mouth. These bars are easy to make and a perfect dessert for any party gathering.

Ingredients

- *1 cup cold butter, cubed*
- *½ cup sugar*
- *1 cup all-purpose flour*
- *1 cup almond flour*
- *A pinch of salt*
- *3 egg yolks*
- *14 oz sweetened condensed milk*

- ¾ cup lime juice
- ½ tbsp rum extract
- 20 mint leaves
- Powdered sugar

Directions

- Preheat the oven to 350°F.
- Add the butter, sugar, all-purpose flour, almond flour, and salt to a food processor and process until well combined.
- Spread the shortbread dough evenly on a baking sheet lined with parchment paper. It should be about 1 inch thick.
- Bake the shortbread for 20 minutes (or less if you have a thinner layer of the dough).
- Meanwhile, add the egg yolks, condensed milk, lime juice, rum extract, and mint leaves to the food processor and pulse into a smooth puree.
- Pour the puree over the baked shortbread and bake for 20 minutes.
- Let the shortbread cool completely, then cut into bars.
- Sprinkle the shortbread bars with powdered sugar, then serve.

Nutrition-Per Serving: Calories: 284Kcal, Total Fat: 20g, Total Carbs: 20g, Protein: 4g

Coconut Balls with Chocolate

| Prep time: 15 min | Cook time: 10 min | Servings: 4 |

Sometimes you only need simple ingredients to make a delectable dessert. These coconut balls have a sweet coconut center covered with a chocolate coating. You will not get enough of them.

Ingredients

- ½ *cup sweetened condensed milk*
- *1 ½ cups shredded coconut*
- ⅛ *tsp vanilla*
- ⅓ *cup honey*
- *6 oz melted chocolate (or more, as needed)*

Directions

- Add condensed milk and coconut to a skillet.

- Cook the coconut mixture over medium heat for about 10 minutes until it thickens.
- Turn off the heat and let the coconut mixture cool slightly.
- Roll out the coconut mixture into balls and place them on a baking sheet lined with parchment paper.
- Place the coconut balls in a freezer for 20 minutes to cool completely.
- Meanwhile, add honey and chocolate to a saucepan and cook for 3 minutes, until it mixes together well.
- Dip the coconut balls into the honey mixture.
- If desired, you may coat the balls with additional coconut flakes, cocoa powder, or sugar!

Nutrition-Per Serving: Calories: 143Kcal, Total Fat: 1g, Total Carbs: 39g, Protein: 1g

Baked Apple Empanadas

| Prep time: 1 h 25 min | Cook time: 30 min | Servings: 8 |

The sweet aroma of the apple empanada filling, which spreads through the kitchen as it bakes, makes them irresistible. They are delicious.

Ingredients

- 3 cups all-purpose flour
- ½ cup sugar
- 1 pinch salt
- 1 cup cold butter, cubed
- 2 eggs
- 2 tbsp cold water
- 1 egg white
- 4 tbsp brown sugar

For the Filling

- *5 apples, peeled and cut into pieces*
- *¾ cup brown sugar*
- *1 tbsp lemon juice*
- *¼ tbsp vanilla extract*
- *⅛ tbsp ground cinnamon*
- *⅛ tbsp ground cloves*

Directions

- Add all the filling ingredients to a saucepan.
- Cook the filling over medium-high heat for 20 minutes while stirring occasionally.
- Meanwhile, add flour, sugar, salt, butter, eggs, and water to a food processor and process until well combined.
- Transfer the dough to a floured surface and divide it into 16 balls. Roll out each ball into 6 inches diameter using a rolling pin. Cover the dough and set it aside for 30 minutes.
- Preheat the oven to 375°F.
- Place 2 spoonful of the filling in the center of each dough and fold them to seal. Make a small cut at the top of each empanada.
- Place the empanadas on a baking sheet and brush them with egg whites.
- Sprinkle the empanadas with sugar and bake them for 30 minutes.
- Tip: serve with a scoop of vanilla ice cream and enjoy.

Nutrition-Per Serving: Calories: 281Kcal, Total Fat: 12g, Total Carbs: 37g, Protein: 4g

Rice Pudding

| Prep time: 5 min | Cook time: 45 min | Servings: 8 |

Rice pudding is a guaranteed way of satisfying your sweet cravings. Even better, you can enjoy the pudding while hot or cold.

Ingredients

- *1 cup long grain rice*
- *2 cinnamon sticks*
- *A pinch of salt*
- *2 ½ cup water*
- *4 cups milk*
- *1 cup granulated sugar*
- *Ground cinnamon*

Directions

- Add rice, cinnamon, salt, and water to a skillet and bring the mixture to a boil over high heat.
- Reduce the heat to low and cook the rice for about 15 minutes until most water has been absorbed.
- Stir in the milk to the rice and cook for 15 more minutes as you stir occasionally.
- Add sugar to the rice and mix. Cook for 10 minutes while stirring often. Raise the heat to medium-high and cook the pudding for an additional 5 minutes.
- Turn off the heat and let the rice pudding cool for at least 15 minutes.
- Garnish the pudding with cinnamon and serve.

Nutrition-Per Serving: Calories: 242Kcal, Total Fat: 3g, Total Carbs: 50g, Protein: 7g

Pumpkin Flan

| Prep time: 10 min | Cook time: 1 h 10 min | Servings: 6 |

It is pumpkin season and you are wondering how to utilize the pumpkins? Make pumpkin flans for your guests. You will get thumbs up as they come for more.

Ingredients

For the Custard Mixture

- ¼ cup granulated sugar
- 12 oz evaporated milk
- 14 oz condensed milk
- 3 tbsp cream cheese
- 1 cup pumpkin puree
- 5 eggs

- *1 tbsp cornstarch*
- *A pinch of cinnamon*
- *½ tbsp vanilla extract*

For the Caramel Mixture

- *1 cup granulated sugar*
- *¼ cup water*
- *⅛ tbsp cream of tartar*

Directions

- Add all the custard mixture to a bowl and mix until well combined. Set aside.
- Preheat the oven to 300°F. Prepare a flan mold.
- Add the caramel ingredients to a saucepan and cook over medium heat for 3 minutes while stirring constantly.
- Increase the heat to medium-high and cook the syrup for 10 minutes.
- Pour the caramel into molds and swirl it around to coat.
- Pour the custard mixture over the molds.
- Arrange the mold in a deep roasting pan and pour over 1 cup of boiling water.
- Bake the pumpkin flan for about 60 minutes.
- Let the pumpkin flan cool for 30 minutes before inverting it on a platter.
- Serve and enjoy.

Nutrition-Per Serving: Calories: 408Kcal, Total Fat: 24g, Total Carbs: 32g, Protein: 18g

Printed in Great Britain
by Amazon